WELCOME TO HUNTLY CA[STLE]

This is a noble ruin in a beautiful setting, remarkable both for the quality of its architecture and for its eventful history.

In medieval times, Aberdeenshire was truly 'Gordon Country' and Huntly Castle, the family's ancient seat, mirrors the rise and decline of the Gordons.

The surviving remains also reveal the story of the development of the castle in Scotland, from the motte and bailey of the 1100s, through the tower house of the later middle ages, to the stately stone palace of the Jacobean era.

Above: A boar's head, carved on the south front of the castle, welcomes visitors to Huntly. The boar's head was a heraldic device of the Gordon family.

CONTENTS

HIGHLIGHTS 2

EXPLORE

Explore Huntly Castle 4
The development of the castle 6
The motte and exterior of the palace 8
The palace remodelled 10
The loggia, east range and ravelin 12
The tower house and courtyard buildings 14
The frontispiece 16
The palace interior 18
  The basement and ground floor 19
  The first floor 20
  The second floor 22

HISTORY

The history of Huntly Castle and the Gordons 24
The Wars of Independence 26
The rise of the Gordons 28
The 'Cock o' the North' 30
The marquisate of Huntly 32
The final years 34

DISCOVER HISTORIC SCOTLAND 36

HISTORIC SCOTLAND MEMBERSHIP 37

FURTHER READING 37

[L]eft: Part of the magnificent frontispiece over the main [d]oorway of the castle, described as 'probably the most [sp]lendid heraldic doorway in the British Isles'.

HUNTLY CASTLE AT A GLANCE

The impressive medieval castle at Huntly was initially built for an earl of Fife in the late 1100s, but later became the chief residence of the mighty Gordon family.

Right: The south front of Huntly Castle, drawn by Robert Billings in 1845.

The great inscription placed on the palace by the 1st Marquis of Huntly around 1600 triumphantly proclaims the family's importance. Yet even as the masons were erecting it, the sands were shifting under the Gordons' edifice of power.

The family's rise to power in north-east Scotland began in 1314 when Sir Adam de Gordon, a Berwickshire nobleman, received the lands and castle of Strathbogie. A descendant was to build a large tower house in the bailey.

By degrees, the family relocated to a splendid new palace, adjacent to the tower. The downfall in the family's fortunes is poignantly encapsulated in the palace's ruinous east range, the construction of which was abruptly halted by the civil wars of the mid-1600s and the execution of the 2nd Marquis.

EARLS AND MARQUISES

25 DUNCAN, EARL OF FIFE

Granted Strathbogie by King William I in the late 1100s.

30 GEORGE GORDON, 4TH EARL OF HUNTLY

Earl George entertained Marie of Guise at Huntly in 1556, but died fighting her daughter, Mary Queen of Scots, in 1562.

34 GEORGE GORDON, 2ND MARQUIS OF HUNTLY

The 2nd Marquis died in 1649 for loyally supporting Charles I.

NOBLE BUILDINGS

6 MOTTE AND BAILEY CASTLE

The s of Fife built the formidable motte and bailey castle in the 1100s.

14 GREAT TOWER HOUSE

The Gordons built a great tower house as their residence around 1400. James VI blew it up in 1594.

9 RENAISSANCE PALACE

The 6th Earl stunningly redesigned the palace to mark his creation as 1st Marquis of Huntly in 1599.

EXQUISITE DETAILS

10 INSCRIPTION

The most striking feature of the entire castle. Look out for the hand of God.

16 FRONTISPIECE

The sculpture over the palace's front door is a feast of heraldry and iconography.

22 INTERIOR DECOR

The fireplaces and plaster fragments in the palace show just how lavishly decorated this remarkable building was.

EVERYDAY LIFE

21 TOILET SEAT

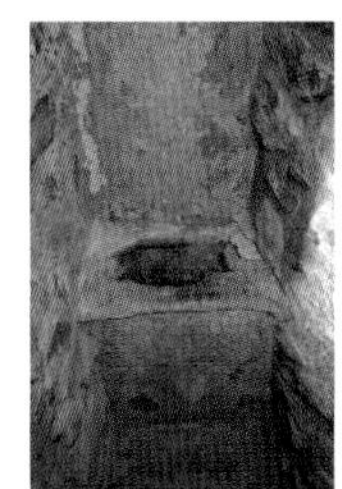

Huntly Castle must have one of the oldest latrine closets in Scotland.

15 BREWERY

The castle had to cater for a large retinue of servants – each drank about a gallon of beer a day!

19 GRAFFITI

You can see scenes of everyday life scratched into plaster in the palace cellars, perhaps by the servants working 'below stairs'.

1
2
3
4
5
6
7
8
9
10

1

2

3

4

EXPLORE HUNTLY CASTLE

Huntly Castle was an important stronghold of the 1100s, which over time was transformed into a palatial residence for a great nobleman. The physical remains of the castle, although fascinating, are also complex.

On the next two pages, therefore, is a glimpse at the four main phases of the castle's development to help you understand what survives.

A good place to begin exploring is beside the grass-covered motte, the oldest part of the castle. After that, you can discover the exterior of the castle and the courtyard buildings, and the interior of the imposing palace.

Opposite: An artist's bird's-eye view of the castle from the east.

Below: Part of the south front of the castle from the south-east, showing the great round tower.

Illustration key

1 Motte (late 1100s)
2 Palace (mid-1400s–early 1600s)
3 Loggia (early 1600s)
4 East Range (early 1600s)
5 Roadway (? 1400s)
6 Ravelin (early 1600s)
7 Brewhouse and bakehouse (1500s)
8 Outbuildings (? 1400s)
9 Tower house (early 1400s)
10 Stable (? early 1600s)

THE DEVELOPMENT OF THE CASTLE

Above: Huntly's three castles. In the background is the motte, built in the 1190s. The bailey housed the later castles: the stone tower house, built around 1400, and the palace, first built around 1460, remodelled in the 1550s and added to in about 1600.

THE MOTTE AND BAILEY CASTLE

1100s

The first castle, built of timber, rose above substantial earthworks. It was sited at an important river crossing and exploited a natural mound. The main elements were a motte (mound), where the lord's residence was, and a bailey (courtyard), which housed the great hall, chapel and stables, among other buildings.

THE TOWER HOUSE AND PALACE

Early 1400s

The timber building on the motte was abandoned as the lord's residence and replaced by a large stone L-plan tower house in the north-west corner of the bailey. Shortly afterwards, a new stone-built great hall was constructed beside it, along the south side of the bailey, together with other less substantial buildings.

THE REMODELLING OF THE PALACE

Mid-1500s

The great hall built in the early 1400s was extensively remodelled above the level of the lower basement, and increased in height. This enlarged palace replaced the tower house as the lord's residence. A substantial west range linked the palace and tower house.

THE TWILIGHT OF THE CASTLE

Early 1600s

The palace was again transformed, creating the stunning building we admire today. The west range was rebuilt, and an east range was in the process of being constructed although it remained unfinished. The tower house had been rendered uninhabitable in 1594, though the extent of its ruination is not clear. It is now believed that the tower house remained as a substantial ruin into the 1700s.

THE MOTTE

The motte and bailey of the first castle at Huntly survive as modest grassy mounds.

The earthworks were created from a low natural mound overlooking the point where the rivers Bogie and Deveron meet, an important crossing place. The motte's grassy summit once provided an elevated position for the lord's residence, ringed by a defensive timber palisade.

Although the motte was in time abandoned, it remained a significant feature of the castle, perhaps demonstrating the ancient lineage of the castle's owners.

Above: The main part of the castle stood on this small mound in the 1100s.

THE PALACE EXTERIOR

The palace is one of Scotland's most impressive medieval buildings, and this south front one of its most remarkable features.

The inscription at the top proudly proclaims the status of the marquis and marchioness of Huntly as owners. The date on that inscription – 1602 – refers only to a major refurbishment of the building, not to its construction, which began around 1450 to complement the accommodation in the great tower house in the courtyard beyond (see pages 14–15).

The original palace probably housed a great hall on an upper floor with a private chamber in the projecting round tower. The design may have been French-inspired, since lodgings with attached single towers were fashionable there in late-medieval times, such as Suscinio in Brittany, built in the 1330s, which bears a striking resemblance to Huntly.

The original palace was extensively remodelled in the 1550s to create a more suitable noble lodging than that provided by the tower house. Apart from the basement, the rest of the palace was almost completely rebuilt, and the whole building raised by a storey to allow separate lodgings for the earl and his countess. Again the design seems to have been inspired by French chateaux – we know that the 4th Earl visited France in 1550, in the retinue of Queen Marie of Guise.

Above: A keyhole gun loop dating to the later 1400s.

Opposite: The south façade of the palace at Huntly Castle is one of the finest pieces of late medieval secular architecture in Scotland.

THE PALACE REMODELLED

The palace was further remodelled by George Gordon, the 6th Earl, following his elevation to the marquisate of Huntly in 1599. Although he did not significantly alter the internal planning, the earl greatly enhanced the appearance of the palace, most spectacularly its south front.

This work too is strikingly French in character. Like his grandfather, the 1st Marquis travelled to France, first as a student then as an exile. He must have been greatly influenced by the various chateaux he visited and stayed in.

It is unlikely, however, that one in particular served as a model for his reconstruction – the windows here seem very much a fusion of French and Scottish styles. While the double-height dormer windows could have been borrowed from a number of French châteaux, such as Bonnivet, near Poitiers, the oriel windows (a type of bay window on upper storeys) are reminiscent of other Scottish examples, including those at the royal palaces of Edinburgh and Linlithgow, dating from the 1400s, and at the near-contemporary Earl's Palace in Kirkwall, Orkney.

Above: The great inscription on the south front of the castle (reproduced in full, below) proclaimed the rise of the Gordons from earls to marquises.

Below: Hands point to both lines of the inscription; a man's for the top line and a lady's (shown here) for the bottom one.

GEORGE GORDOVN FIRST MARQVIS OF HVNTLIE 16
HENRIETTE STEWART MARQVESSE OF HVNTLIE 02

Although the palace reveals both French and Scottish influences, the first marquis's prime intention was probably to create a classical building. The scale and prominence of the inscription across the topmost windows, as well as the use of Roman lettering, indicates that the marquis was looking to classical exemplars. However, the inscription is carved in relief rather than incised into the stone, as was more usual with classical examples; perhaps the craftsman responsible for the work may only have had knowledge of such antique friezes through drawings, which would give no indication of an inscription's character.

We are fortunate that a series of sketches made by the artist John Claude Nattes in 1799 survives, showing the palace substantially complete. One sketch clearly shows the high pitched roof, and the sumptuous oriel windows rising through two storeys and terminating in gableted dormers. The great round tower has a high conical roof, and fine dormer windows lighting the roof space. An elaborate oriel rises from the front below the wall walk with heavy mouldings continuing round the top of the tower. To the east would have been a rectangular two-storey turret balancing the round tower, but this had already collapsed by 1799.

Above: French castles such as Bonnivet may have provided a model for some details at Huntly, such as the windows.

Above: The inspiration for Huntly's oriel windows, such as this one, may have come from home-grown sources such as Edinburgh Castle.

Left: John Claude Nattes sketched the south front of the palace in 1799, when much of the building was still roofed.

THE LOGGIA

The loggia, a covered arcade, provided an open but sheltered place from which the family and house guests might view the formal gardens. The room above, accessible from the palace, also provided fine views.

The loggia was probably built by the second marquis, who spent the late 1630s and early 1640s adding to his ancestral seat, although we do not know if he was initiating his own building projects or simply completing works begun by his father. (The 1st Marquis was employing Ralf Raleine, a carver, at the palace as late as 1633.)

Only the pier bases carrying the arcade survive, but in the 1790s the structure was described as something remarkable: 'many people … remember to have seen a range of pillars, supporting an arched roof … intended as a cover for such as inclined to take the aire, or a view of the garden … there being a door that led to it from the upper hall.'

There was a vogue for loggias in Scotland and England from the late 1500s. The first marquis probably added a loggia at another of his residences, Bog o' Gight, near Fochabers. A fine ground-floor example survives at Castle Campbell, in Clackmannanshire, built by the 7th Earl of Argyll, a contemporary of Huntly.

Above: The loggia at Huntly may have resembled the first-floor loggias at the now demolished Bog o' Gight (also known as Gordon Castle), probably built by the 1st Marquis of Huntly.

Left: All that remains of the loggia, which must have been a very impressive feature of Huntly's south frontage, are the bases of the columns.

THE EAST RANGE AND RAVELIN

The castle was probably always approached from the east, although the cobbled roadway you see here shows that the alignment was altered in the 1600s, when the present east range and entrance gateway were added.

Above: The east range, in the foreground, was probably the work of the 2nd Marquis but it was never completed: the wars of the mid-1600s permanently interrupted its construction.

The grassy earthwork in the trees beyond the gateway is a ravelin, a form of artillery defence built during the civil wars in the 1640s, when family seats such as Huntly were once again pressed into defensive service. The mound of earth protected cannon placed in front of the castle from incoming cannonballs.

Above: The ravelin resembles the earthwork defences of the earliest castles, but it was one of Huntly Castle's latest features, erected to defend the castle against artillery fire.

The east range, with its projecting entrance porch, was the last major addition to the castle, and must have been the building work referred to in 1643 when a visiting clergyman noted that the second marquis 'was much taken up with his new buildings'.

The plain raised margins to the windows and quoins, or cornerstones, and the finely moulded bases at the entrance, are unlikely to be earlier than this date. A similar detail from the loggia suggests that it was part of the same building programme.

The range seems never to have been completed, probably because the marquis was caught up in the civil wars, paying for his loyalty to Charles I on the scaffold.

Above: The foundations of the tower house, built to an L-plan in the early 1400s.

THE TOWER HOUSE AND COURTYARD BUILDINGS

The most significant building in the courtyard, other than the palace, is the shattered remnant of a great L-plan tower house. This is probably the 'auld werk' that was blown up by James VI in 1594, according to contemporary accounts.

Although now reduced to its foundations, the tower's plan and massive nature show it to be typical of the 1400s. It was probably built either for Sir John Gordon (died 1408), last in the male line of the Gordons of Huntly, or more likely for his brother-in-law, Sir Alexander Seton, who succeeded him through marriage. The tower seems to have been the first masonry building erected on the site. It replaced a timber residence on the motte.

From our knowledge of other tower houses, we can guess at its general arrangements. The vaulted ground floor would have been used for storage. The small chamber in the wing, however, does not appear to have been linked by a doorway to the main block and may therefore have been a prison accessed from above.

The first floor contained the lord's hall in the main block and a side chamber in the wing, which had a fireplace and was large enough to accommodate 15 people.

The tower house was surrounded and served by various ancillary buildings. Some survive as foundations; others to a more substantial height. They include a brewhouse, with the seating of the vat still surviving, and a bakehouse, with two domed ovens. Together these provided the castle household with its staple diet of bread and ale. In the centre of the courtyard are the foundations of a stable with space for ten stalls.

The west side of the courtyard was bounded by a range that probably replaced a stretch of perimeter wall linking the tower house and palace. The range seems to have begun as a less substantial lean-to, which was subsequently enlarged. The scars of rooflines on the palace wall show that the range was two-storeyed in height, whilst the footings of a large, half-round staircase projecting midway along it indicate that the range was of some quality. The ground floor was evidently given over to service activities for there is a bakehouse at the end beside the tower house.

Above: This outline marks where the vat in the brewhouse would sit. Brewhouses and bakehouses were standard features of medieval castles, providing a staple diet of bread and ale.

Below: This plan shows the range of outbuildings that would once have served all the needs of the Gordon family.

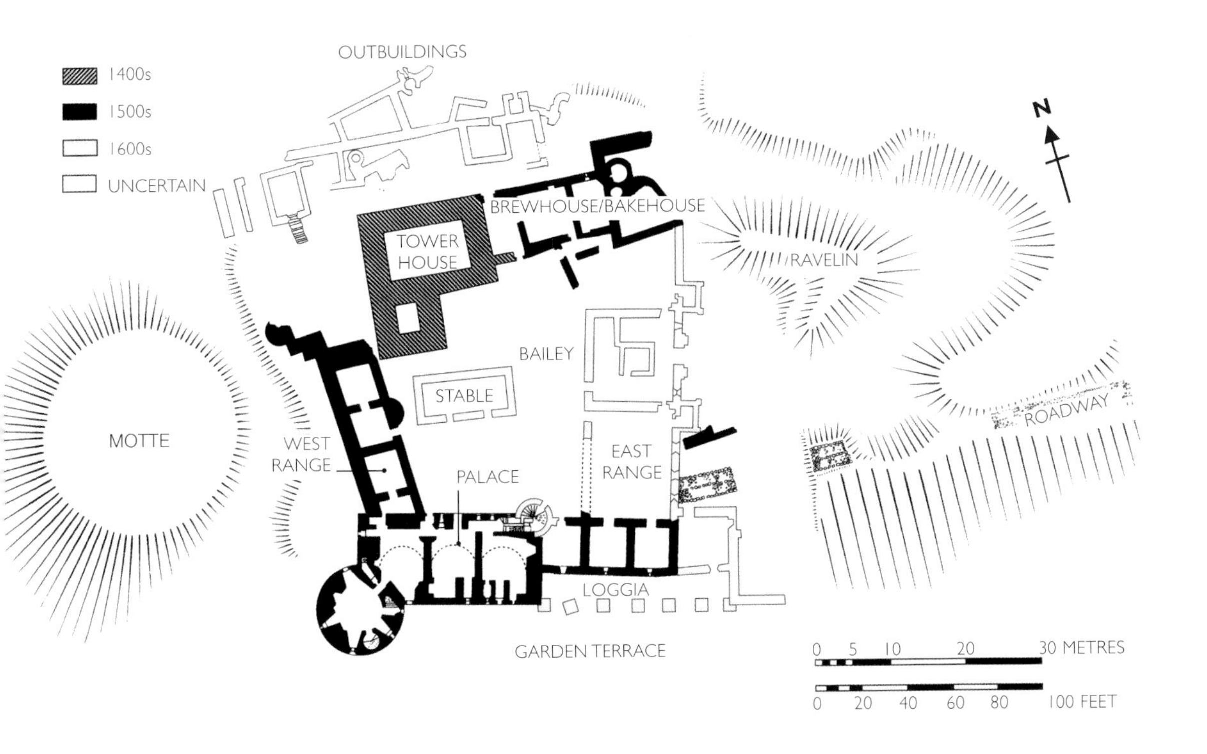

THE FRONTISPIECE

The majestic palace along the south side of the castle now dominates the courtyard at the centre.

Near the top, you can still see a sculptured stone displaying the coat of arms of George Gordon, 4th Earl of Huntly (see page 30). The armorial confirms that it was this earl who rebuilt the palace in the 1550s, raising the roof a full storey in the process.

Above: The first panel of the frontispiece, containing the coat of arms of the 1st Marquis and Marchioness of Huntly.

The magnificent heraldic frontispiece was constructed by the first marquis about 50 years later to impress visitors as they entered. Without parallel in the British Isles, it would have been even more spectacular when first completed with its coats of arms and other details gilded and brightly painted.

The doorway itself is an elaborate Renaissance confection, its lintel (horizontal stone) resting on slim classical pilasters (columns) and ornamented with grotesque animals and heraldry. Directly above is a panel emblazoned with the arms of the marquis and marchioness. As the eye is drawn upwards, it is led successively to higher themes. Above the marquis's coat of arms are those of his sovereigns, James VI and Queen Anna of Denmark. Higher still are two panels which once illustrated the Passion and Resurrection of Christ.

The lower contained the *Arma Christi* (the arms of Christ); the pierced heart, hands and feet, along with the instruments of his Passion. The circular panel above depicted the Risen Christ. The whole composition is crowned by the figure of the warrior archangel Michael triumphing over Satan, representing the victory of Good over Evil on the Day of the Last Judgement.

The meaning of this symbolism would have been clear to the marquis's aristocratic peers. Although the heraldry proclaims the Gordons' loyalty to the monarchy and to God, the religious symbolism was a declaration of the marquis's own Catholic faith.

This was a dangerously bold declaration to make in a predominantly Protestant post-Reformation Scotland, which only a man as powerful and as well connected as the Marquis of Huntly dared to do. The religious imagery of the frontispiece was carefully defaced when the Covenanters occupied the castle in the 1640s. They left the earthly heraldry untouched.

Opposite: The frontispiece was a stunning heraldic creation that would have originally been tinctured with coloured pigments. It would have been the visual focus of the courtyard.

THE PALACE INTERIOR

Above: A cutaway illustration showing how the palace might have looked in about 1599. The basement was divided into cellars and, in the round tower, probably a prison. The ground floor housed the kitchens and steward's room; the first and second floors the marquis and marchioness's respective apartments. The attic floor contained bedrooms.

THE BASEMENT

The basement is divided into three storage cellars. Each has a polygonal-headed doorway and is lit by an 'inverted-keyhole' gunhole, features characteristic of the later 1400s.

The basement of the round tower is reached along a narrow passage built in the thickness of the wall. This passage would have been secured by doors at either end, with the opening into the tower held fast by a set of double doors.

The basement of the tower has all the feel of a very bleak medieval pit-prison. However, it has no latrine, most unusual even for a pit-prison. The chamber originally had an intermediate floor of timber, probably with a hatch giving access to the lower level. If it were a prison, unfortunates would have been thrown down into the pit, with the upper floor perhaps a slightly less harsh place of confinement. Alternatively, both floors could have served the rather more mundane purpose of a fire-proof strongroom for the earls' documents, charters, plate and other valuables.

Above: Looking through the great doorway to the stair.

Above: Graffiti of a man with a sword, on the wall of the palace cellars, perhaps drawn by servants at an idle moment.

THE GROUND FLOOR

This level was the service floor of the palace, comprising a kitchen flanked by two rooms. The kitchen was well fitted out with a large fireplace and a freshwater supply and waste outlet through the north wall, the medieval equivalent of the kitchen sink with built-in waste disposal.

The rooms to either side were originally storage or preparation rooms, but at some point were converted into living spaces, each with a fireplace; the west room also has a latrine. The room in the round tower was likewise a private chamber, again with a latrine (still with its wooden seat) and a fireplace and lit by large south-facing windows.

This room probably accommodated a senior member of the household such as the steward, since it had two staircases; one leading directly up to the lord's private chamber, to which it was also linked by a bell-pull system, and another to the great chamber.

Above: The prison was secured by outward-opening doors.

THE FIRST FLOOR

The first floor formed the earl's apartments, the most prestigious rooms in the castle. They owe much of their stately appearance to the first marquis, who embellished them, but the general arrangement and sequence of rooms dates to the earlier reconstruction by the 4th Earl.

A document entitled *The Maner of the Erles of Huntlies Death* (1576) provides full details of the layout. After suffering a stroke during a game of football, the 5th Earl was carried dying into his own chamber and laid in his bed, 'quhilk was ane round within the grit chalmer' – that is, a round chamber beyond the great chamber. The great chamber is also referred to as the 'chalmer of daice' (dais chamber) and had two doors, the 'chalmer durre' leading to the earl's bedchamber and 'the utter [outer] chalmer durre', which presumably led out to the hall.

This three-roomed arrangement – hall, outer or great chamber and inner or bedchamber – was common in late medieval times, and one that the first marquis retained. The sequence created a hierarchy of spaces, with only the most intimate of friends and advisors gaining access to the lord's bedchamber.

Above: The first floor hall, the least restricted of the reception rooms for visitors who wished to see the earl. It also served as a dining room.

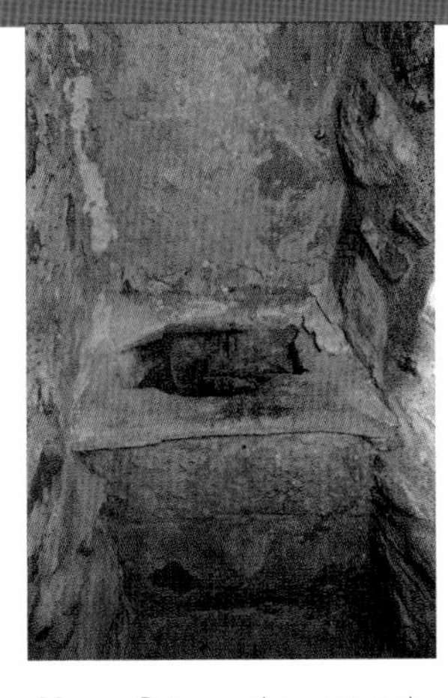

Above: Between the great and the inner chambers on the first floor was the earl's latrine closet. The toilet seat, pictured, is one of the oldest to survive in Scotland.

The apartment now appears rather stark, the rooms having been stripped of their fireplaces and most of their decoration. However, they remain impressive spaces, and enough survives to hint at their lost grandeur. The remains of a fine plaster ceiling cornice can be seen in both the hall and great chamber. More intimately, the earl's toilet seat still remains in the closet between the great and inner chambers.

Later visitors to the castle mention the splendid decoration of the rooms. In 1780 the writer and clergyman Charles Cordiner observed that 'some of the apartments, and in particular the curious ceilings, are still preserved pretty entire. They are painted with a variety of subjects, in small divisions… In these the virtues, vices, trades and pursuits of mankind are characterised by emblematic figures.' This reference to painted timber ceilings accords with our knowledge that in 1617 the painter John Anderson was summoned from Huntly to carry out work at Falkland Palace and Edinburgh Castle. He may have been the craftsman responsible for the painted decoration noted by Cordiner.

THE MISSING CHAPEL

The Gordons were devout Catholics and had a chapel prominently placed in their palace. A chapel dedicated to St Mary is recorded in 1508, and in 1607 the first marquis was reportedly rebuilding it. Cordiner, visiting in 1780, recalled an ornate chapel with a ceiling decorated with representations of sacred subjects and the parables. But where was it? The most likely location was on the first floor of the ruined range attached to the east end of the palace. Accessible both from the marquis's apartment and the main stair, the upper floor of the range may well have been an ante-room with a chapel beyond. The rooms are orientated correctly for a chapel (east–west), and were obviously of some distinction as there is evidence of a sprung wooden floor above the ground-floor vault.

Below: These slight remains of a once fine plaster ceiling on the first floor give some impression of the now-lost splendour of the palace.

THE SECOND FLOOR

The second floor was the countess's apartment. It was a mirror image of the earl's apartment below, with a sequence of hall, great chamber and inner chamber, together with a toilet closet.

However, the whole appearance was embellished during the first marquis's 'make over' around 1600. The building was once again heightened, and the south wall given graceful oriel windows, affording spectacular views over the gardens and grounds.

The fireplaces were also made more elaborate, with wonderfully decorated stone mantelpieces that would have sparkled with heraldic colours. Yellow paint with black, brown and red designs still survives on the few patches of plaster.

As with the frontispiece, the hall fireplace is carved with a mixture of heraldic devices and religious symbolism, with classical details, including columns and obelisks, framing the panels. The panel at the top, its contents carefully chiselled off, doubtless once contained religious imagery seen as idolatrous by the Covenanters.

The fireplace in the marchioness's great chamber is somewhat more homely, as befits the more intimate space. The lintel has carved medallion portraits of the marquis and marchioness, together with their arms and mottoes.

The small service stair between the marchioness's great chamber and bedchamber passes by the attic floor, which is no longer accessible but had additional bedrooms, perhaps for junior members of the family.

The stair leads to the wallhead with its small, octagonal belvedere, or turret. Look out and try to imagine the wonderful gardens and grounds that would have stretched before you 400 years ago.

The fine avenue of lime trees along which you approached the castle was planted about 200 years ago, after the castle had been abandoned. However, it may have replaced an earlier avenue, for an outer gatehouse stood at the far end until 1839, when it was demolished to make way for the construction of the Gordon Schools, financed by the fifth duke of Gordon's widow.

Opposite: The great fireplace in the hall of the marchioness's lodging. Covenanters chiselled off the fireplace's religious imagery, although they left this verse from Romans 8:28 intact:
'Sen God doth us defend
ve sal prevail unto the end.
To thaes that love God
Al thingis virkis to the best.'

Above: Medallion portraits of George Gordon (top), the 1st Marquis, and Henrietta Stewart, the 1st Marchioness, sculpted on the fireplace in the marchioness's great chamber.

THE HISTORY OF
HUNTLY CASTLE AND THE GORDONS

When the first castle was built at Strathbogie (now Huntly) in the 1100s, Scotland was undergoing a period of profound change in Scotland.

David I and his grandsons, Malcolm IV and William I, transformed the kingdom along European lines, inviting colonists to settle and build castles to defend their new territories.

While there was resistance to David and his successors' rule, the conflict was not necessarily a struggle between the 'old' Celtic and the 'new' feudal Scotland. The most determined resistance came from the dynastic challenges of the rulers of the semi-independent province of Moray. Although David and his grandsons very much depended upon their newly settled supporters to counter these threats, it is now thought that native earls played an important role in extending the Crown's authority in the north.

These native earls included Earl Duncan (II) of Fife, granted the estate of Strathbogie as a reward for serving William I in his campaigns against the MacWilliams of Moray. Duncan probably built the motte and bailey that underlies the later stone castle, calling it the Peel of Strathbogie. In 1204, when David de Strathbogie, Earl Duncan's third son, inherited the northern estates, Strathbogie became his headquarters.

The Fifes of Strathbogie later became earls of Atholl when David's grandson, also David, acquired the earldom through marriage in 1264. He died six years later at Tunis while on Louis IX of France's ill-fated crusade. John de Strathbogie, who succeeded Earl David, supported Robert the Bruce and was executed in London in 1306 for opposing Edward I of England – the first Scottish earl to be executed for 200 years.

Above: The first castle at Huntly was built at the junction of the Bogie and the Deveron rivers.

Opposite: George Gordon, the 2nd Marquis of Huntly.

TIMELINE

c.1190

THE FIRST CASTLE

William I (from whose reign this coin dates) grants Earl Duncan (II) of Fife the estate of Strathbogie.

1270

CRUSADER

David de Strathbogie, Earl of Atholl, dies on crusade in North Africa.

THE WARS OF INDEPENDENCE

For such an important castle, the Peel of Strathbogie appears to have had a surprisingly minor role in Scotland's Wars of Independence with England.

Robert the Bruce, now Robert I, visited in 1307, during his bloody campaign against his arch-opponents, the Comyns. After falling ill at Inverurie he was brought to the security of Strathbogie. On his recovery, Robert went on to rout the Comyns at the battle of Inverurie and thereafter ravage their heartland north of Strathbogie (the act known as 'the herschip of Buchan'), effectively destroying the family's political and military power.

Above: The Gordon lords fought bravely for Scotland during conflicts with England in the 1300s. Sir Alexander Gordon, for example, died during the battle of Neville's Cross (shown here), which took place near Durham on 17 October 1346.

David de Strathbogie, the new Earl of Atholl, perhaps motivated by family links with the Comyns, was unlucky or foolish enough to turn against Robert I just as the king had his greatest triumph at Bannockburn in 1314. David lost his lands and titles as punishment, while Robert granted Strathbogie to a loyal supporter, Sir Adam Gordon de Huntly, in Berwickshire.

Yet it was not until 1376, when the line of the Strathbogie earls of Atholl finally died out, that Sir Adam Gordon de Huntly and his heirs could feel secure in their new northern lands. Until then the Gordons appear to have focused on their Berwickshire estates. They were stalwart patriots in the conflict with England, and successive Gordon lords paid the price with their lives: Sir Adam at Halidon Hill, near Berwick, in 1333, Sir Alexander at Neville's Cross, near Durham, in 1346, Sir John at Otterburn, Northumberland, in 1388, and a second Sir Adam in 1402, leading a charge at Homildon Hill in Northumberland.

In 1408 Sir John Gordon, son of Adam and last in the male line of the Gordons of Huntly and Strathbogie, died and was succeeded by his sister, Elizabeth, who that same year married Sir Alexander Seton. He succeeded to the lordship and in about 1437 is believed to have been created Lord Gordon by James I. It was probably Seton who, in the desire to stamp his authority on his lands, built the great stone tower house in the bailey of the old castle, replacing the residence on the motte that had served for over 200 years.

1314

THE GORDONS ARRIVE

Robert the Bruce grants Strathbogie to Sir Adam Gordon de Huntly.

1436

LORD GORDON

Alexander, created Lord Gordon, builds a great tower house.

THE RISE OF THE GORDONS

After Bruce's defeat of the Comyns, the Gordons rapidly became the most powerful family in north-east Scotland, thanks to their loyal support of the Crown.

Above: The heraldic boar of the Gordon family, carved into the south front of the palace.

Alexander, 2nd Lord Gordon, was made Earl of Huntly around 1445, and shortly after extended the family's landed interests by acquiring the lordship of Badenoch, with its castle at Ruthven, near Kingussie. In about 1457, he changed the family name from Seton to Gordon, thereby preserving the Gordon lineage.

Alexander loyally supported James II in his bitter conflict with the Black Douglases, and as well as serving as the king's lieutenant in the north-east he married James's sister, Annabella. In 1452 he defeated the Douglas Earl of Crawford at Brechin. But with Alexander so engaged, Archibald Douglas, Earl of Moray, attacked Strathbogie and fired the castle. Alexander hotly pursued Moray, exacting his revenge on the townspeople of Elgin.

Moray's death in battle in 1455, at Erkinholme near Langholm, effectively ended the Black Douglases' power, and Alexander seized this opportunity by capturing the Douglas castles of Darnaway and Lochindorb, and by arranging his son's marriage to Elizabeth Dunbar, widow of the Earl of Moray. The marriage was not a success and ended in divorce, frustrating Huntly's plan to appropriate the wealthy earldom of Moray.

With the demise of the Black Douglases, the earls of Huntly became the undisputed power in the north. This is reflected in a major remodelling of the castle, perhaps required after

c.1445

EARL OF HUNTLY
Alexander, second Lord Gordon, acquires Ruthven Castle. Ruthven Barracks (right), was built on the site of this castle.

1452

GORDONS V. DOUGLASES
During James II's campaign against him, Douglas, Earl of Moray, attacks Huntly Castle.

the 1452 attack. The new building, which now only survives as the basement of the palace, was unfinished when the earl died at Strathbogie in 1470. The work was completed by his son, George, 2nd Earl.

In 1506 Alexander, 3rd Earl, received a charter from James IV allowing him to change the name of his residence from Strathbogie to Huntly. The change was probably suggested by Huntly himself, in an attempt to make the earldom and the castle synonymous. Even so, the name Strathbogie continued into the 1600s.

The loyalty of the Gordons and the grandeur of their castle secured it numerous royal visits. James IV came frequently, and the royal accounts detail the expenses incurred by him on his various visits: they include gaming debts, payments to minstrels and gifts to a Moorish juggler. Two payments of 'drinksilver' to stonemasons, in 1501 and 1505, show that building work was in progress.

Below: The tomb of Alexander Gordon, 1st Earl of Huntly, who died in 1470. The tomb, whose effigy shows the earl in the robe of lord chancellor of Scotland, lies in St Mary's Aisle, Elgin Cathedral.

1496

ENGLISH PRETENDER

Lady Catherine Gordon, the 'White Rose of Scotland', marries Perkin Warbeck, the pretender to the English throne.

1505

ROYAL VISITOR

James IV visits Huntly and pays 'drinksilver' to the stonemasons working there.

THE 'COCK O' THE NORTH'

Under George Gordon, the 4th Earl, the family's authority in the north-east reached its zenith, so much so that he became known as 'Cock o' the North'.

Not only was Gordon chief of the most powerful northern family, but he was also lord chancellor and a nephew of James V through his mother, the natural daughter of James IV. In 1550 the earl travelled to France in the entourage of Queen Marie of Guise, widow of James V. His substantial wealth and foreign travels equipped him with both the means and the motivation to remodel the palace in cosmopolitan fashion, almost from the ground up.

The earl's building project may have befitted a man of his station, but his power and visible wealth were beginning to threaten the very family to which the Gordons had always been loyal – the royal house of Stewart. In 1556 Marie, now queen-regent, visited Huntly. She was entertained so splendidly that, after a few days, she wished to depart so as to relieve the burden on her host. The earl reassured her by displaying the castle's huge vaults full of provisions. In response to such conspicuous wealth, the French ambassador advised Marie that 'the wings of the Cock of the North should be clipped'.

An opportunity for this clipping came in the reign of Marie's daughter, Mary Queen of Scots. The pretext was the earl's continued adherence to Catholicism after the Reformation Act of 1560 had abolished the mass and Scotland's adherence to Rome. Political necessity persuaded Mary, a Catholic herself, to crush the Gordons – by doing so she would show her Protestant lords that she would neither suffer challenges to royal authority nor favour Catholics.

Above: This much-worn armorial panel displays the coat of arms of George, 4th Earl of Huntly, joined with those of his wife, Elizabeth Keith. It was set into the palace during its reconstruction by the fourth earl.

1556

ROYAL VISIT

Queen Marie of Guise visits the 4th Earl at Huntly Castle.

1562

ROYAL WRATH

Mary Queen of Scots defeats the 4th Earl in battle and has his castle looted.

In October 1562 the royal army confronted the earl and his small force at Corrichie, 24 miles (38km) south-east of Huntly Castle. Gordon was captured but later fell from his horse and died. His embalmed corpse was subsequently tried and found guilty of treason in Edinburgh, and his castle ransacked. An inventory taken at the time presents an impressive picture of its wealth and splendour, including all the treasures of Aberdeen Cathedral, which had been packed up and handed over to Huntly for safe-keeping in 1559 to preserve them from the 'cleansings' of radical Protestants. One notable item was the silk tent in which Edward II of England had slept the night before Bannockburn.

Above: The north face of the palace at Huntly, framed by a window in the brewhouse and bakehouse building. This side of the palace is far less showy than the outward-looking southern face, but it does demonstrate changes to the building, carried out by the 4th Earl.

THE MARQUISATE OF HUNTLY

The second half of the 1500s was a turbulent time for the Gordons, as for many of Scotland's noble families.

Almost complete ruin in 1562 was followed by restoration of the family's lands and titles in 1565 to George Gordon, who became the 5th Earl and who remained loyal to Mary during the civil war that followed her flight to England in 1568. When the earl died in 1576, at Huntly Castle, it was from his exertions on the football field and not the battlefield.

George, 6th Earl, had spent his teenage years in France, at the university in Paris and at the court of Henri III. The experience influenced both his religious convictions and his buildings.

Although a favourite of James VI, he constantly tried his monarch's patience through his involvement in numerous ill-conceived and treasonable acts, including the 'Spanish Blanks' plot of 1592, in which he was implicated in a conspiracy with Catholic Spain. In 1594 James VI finally acted against Huntly and his fellow conspirators, the Earls of Errol and Angus, and Huntly was forced to flee to France.

1594

ROYAL REVENGE
James VI puts down the 6th Earl's rebellion and partially destroys Huntly Castle.

1599

ROYAL PARDON
The 6th Earl becomes the 1st Marquis of Huntly and sets about remodelling his palace.

James's anger at his errant earl was taken out on his castle. He seems initially to have been reluctant to destroy it, but was eventually persuaded by his captains to cast down this symbol of Huntly's pride. Two days after the king's arrival, 'nothing was left unhocked [standing] savinge the greate olde tower which shall be blown up with powder.' Despite such reports, the damage can only have been limited, for the palace survived reasonably intact. Even the tower house, which was blown up using powder lent by the burgesses of Aberdeen, survived as a substantial ruin until the 1700s, when Alexander Fraser, a mason, was paid 'for taking down the old tower of Huntly Castle'.

Above: The armorial processional roll of the funeral of George Gordon, 1st Marquis of Huntly, in 1636.

The 6th Earl was only reconciled with James in 1597 after he was received into the Kirk. His personal faith was flexible, however, and he was regarded with suspicion by the Kirk throughout his life. In 1601 the General Assembly arranged regular visitations to Huntly 'to instruct the earl and keep off mass priests', and in 1608 he was excommunicated and imprisoned for holding masses in his house. Despite this, Huntly's close friendship with the king continued, and in 1599 he was created marquis of Huntly, whereupon he embarked on a major programme of repair and embellishment of his damaged residence.

1602

REBUILDING COMPLETED

The castle is repaired and embellished after the destruction caused by James VI.

1636

DEATH OF THE 1ST MARQUIS

The 1st Marquis is buried with great ceremony at Elgin Cathedral, close by his ancestor, the 1st Earl.

THE FINAL YEARS

George Gordon, 2nd Marquis of Huntly, was just as enthusiastic a builder as his father had been.

A visiting clergyman noted in 1643 that he 'was much taken up with his new buildings, from four in the morning until eight at night, standing by his masons, urging their diligences, and directing and judging their work, that he had scarce tyme to eate, or sleep, much less write.'

Above: The approach to the castle. The double avenue of lime trees came into state care in 1925.

Ever the loyal subject, George supported Charles I during the various civil wars that beset the sovereign's reign, sealing his devotion on the scaffold in 1649. 'You may take my head from my shoulders', he told the Covenanters, 'but not my heart from my sovereign.'

Huntly Castle also suffered sorely for his loyalty. The Covenanters occupied it in 1640, and the parson of nearby Rothiemay tells how it 'was preserved from being rifled or defaced, except some emblems and imagerye, which looked somewhat popish and superstitious lycke; and therefor, by the industry of one captain James Wallace, wer hewd and broke doune off the frontispiece of the house; but all the rest of the frontispeece containing Huntly's scutcheon, etc, was left untowched, as it standes to this daye.' Wallace's handiwork can still be seen today.

In 1644 the castle was briefly held by the duke of Montrose, and in 1647 Lord Charles Gordon defended it against General Leslie; his garrison was starved into surrender and savage treatment was subsequently meted out, the men hanged and the officers beheaded.

In 1650 Charles II visited on his way from Peterhead to his coronation at Scone. The castle was occupied by Government troops during the 1745 Jacobite Rising, but by then its days as a noble residence had long passed. In 1923 the Duke of Richmond and Gordon placed the ruin into state care, and in 1925 Sir Leybourne Davidson of Huntly Lodge gifted to the nation the fine tree-lined avenue by which the castle is approached.

Above: A detail from General William Roy's map of Scotland, produced in the 1750s, showing Huntly Castle and Huntly Lodge.

1649

BLOODY END

The 2nd Marquis is executed at Edinburgh for his support of the Royalist cause.

1923

STATE CARE

The Duke of Richmond and Gordon places the ruin in state care.

Huntly Castle is one of over 40 Historic Scotland properties in north-east Scotland, a selection of which is shown below.

Balvenie Castle

At Dufftown on the A941

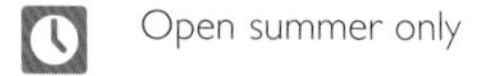

Open summer only

01340 820121

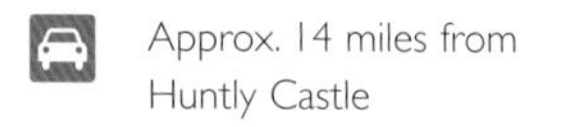

Approx. 14 miles from Huntly Castle

Facilities

Elgin Cathedral

In Elgin on the A96

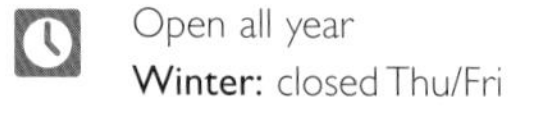

Open all year
Winter: closed Thu/Fri

01343 547171

Approx. 27 miles from Huntly Castle

Facilities

Tolquhon Castle

15m N of Aberdeen on the A920

Open all year
Winter: open weekends only

01651 851286

Approx. 29 miles from Huntly Castle

Facilities

Kildrummy Castle

10m SW of Alford on the A97

Open summer only

01975 571331

Approx. 17 miles from Huntly Castle

Facilities

For more information on all Historic Scotland properties, go to **www.historicenvironment.scot/visit-a-place**

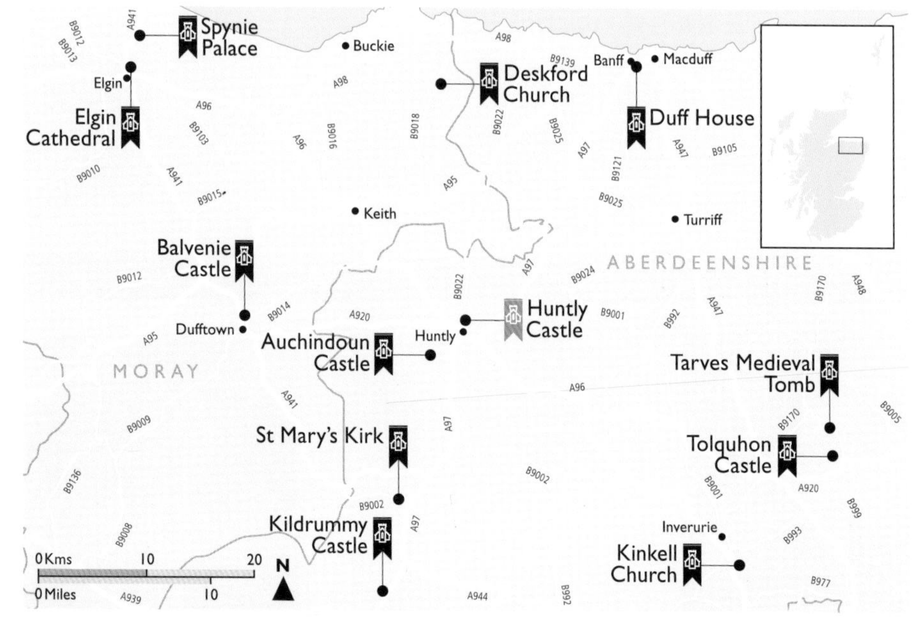